The Assassination Museum

D1331145

Andy Jackson

Red Squirrel Press
(Scotland)

First published in the UK 2010 by
Red Squirrel Press (Scotland)
PO Box 23896
Edinburgh
EH6 9AA

Red Squirrel Press (Head Office)
PO Box 219
Morpeth
NE61 9AU
www.redsquirrelpress.com

Edited by Joanne Cody

ISBN 978-1-906700-16-4

Printed by Martins.

Acknowledgments

Some poems in this collection have previously appeared in other publications, including *Eric, New Writing Dundee, New Writing Scotland, Poetry Scotland, Poetry News, Riverrun* and *The Scotsman*. *Jennie Lee by Robert Capa* was a winner in the National Galleries of Scotland competition 2008.

The author would like to thank the following:- Kevin Cadwallender, Sheila Wakefield and Joanne Cody at Red Squirrel, Colette Bryce, Judith Taylor, Lydia Robb, Dawn Wood, Jim Stewart, Nicole Devarenne, Heather Reid, Colin Will, Sally Evans, Catia Montagna, members of the Soutar House Group and, in particular, Ajay Close for her time and her encouragement.

Illustrations :-

Cover photo 'Dealey Plaza Tilt Shift' reproduced by kind permission of Jan Brašna

Internal photographs by Catia Montagna

For Denise, the best poem I know

Contents

Off The Wall

Boys, if I could give you some advice
it's this; don't wait too long to dance.
3AM, they're kicking on the lights,
don't kid yourself you never got the chance.
At every disco, theories abound -
I'm guilty too – my own research has shown
that sex is codified in sound,
and proved that Sly and the Family Stone
were not related, that Doctor Hook
was not a real doctor. But watch my lips -
the gnostic gospel of the dance - O holy book! -
beatifies the winding of the hips
and castigates mere flexing of the knees,
for they are not the vessel for the soul.
OK, so Orbison could cure disease,
his tears the unctuous oil of rock and roll,
but it was in the dances of communion -
the Time Warp, the Slosh, the Locomotion -
I found the rhythmic blessings of the union,
fell, sated by the raptures of devotion.
I came to that corroboree of perfection
they call the hokey-cokey. It was there
I found my pagan purpose, my connection,
embodied by a credo I could share:
You put your whole self in; your whole self out.
In the end, maybe that's what it's really all about.

The Assassination Museum

In Dallas you can lean through any window
that overlooks the plaza, pull a walking stick
into your shoulder, squeeze until the second breath,

and pick off lonely crypto-fantasists,
Templars and phrenologists, paparazzi on mopeds,
MI6 and monster hunters, ten-a-penny whistleblowers,

those who claim against all sense that they were there,
or know some covert thing we never could.
They gather there in gleeful swarms to sing

their fatal songs, their anthems for the paranoid.
Tune in soon to hear some compelling truths
about the secret *coup d'etat* by ruthless neocons,

or find out how the shadows on the moon that lit the
world
were cast by arc lights in a hidden shed in Idaho.
The King was never dead, and now impersonates
himself.

OK, you got this far. You passed the test. I think we trust
each other.
Now you need to know some things. I can't say what,
but rest assured
that when they come to light they will uncrash the car,
unfire the gun.

If I should die in questionable circumstances, get this poem
to the poet laureate. She'll know what to do.
They're coming for me now. They're at the door. It's up
to you.

Djinn

We sleep in bottles, born of fire
and wait to be uncorked to dance
like moths or filaments of wire,
or curling talons, clawing hands
around your throats. We choke the noise
from bars and back-rooms dark as caves.
Piaf and her shredded voice
are in our breathing sounds, our wails,
her tremolo the rise and fall
of empires. We are dust from dust,
not granting wishes, spurning calls,
we dine on hopes and greed and lust.
We are not slaves to your command,
but flies in amber of the past.
Once carved from dunes of silver sand,
now spirits of the silent glass.

Bric-a-brac

She was raised by vultures, so he said,
the only compliment he ever paid.
It stuck. At rummage sales she probed
the air, sniffing for chrism or perfume
among the reek of stateless clothes and bric-a-brac
between two owners, going out, then coming back
as good or bad as new, but never really cherished.

Her airborne sense drew in the attar
of the flesh – a blouse still reeking, even
through the blasting of the service wash,
a scent she knew, too bold to be subdued.
Yours for a pound, my love. A woman knows
a bargain. *And I'll throw in the onyx dish.*

She recalls an afternoon, infernal and intense,
when, scared, she drenched herself in *Charlie.*
He was sweet, *Old Spice* and chewing gum.
Sunlight from her greedy window
burned a crucifix across his back.
He went home whistling when it was done,
she tidied up but could not wash him off.

Now Mata Hari in the mirror holds
the fraying top across her breasts,
sniffs the bottle, empty since the Silver Jubilee,
and feels him gather, tighten and release.
She pouts and wiggles – *Hello sailor! Come
with me, let's paint the town cerise.*

This Is What She's Like

Sometimes the weather forgets she is there.
She sells home-made jam to fund a face-lift,
there are laws made specifically to deal with her.
She flicks through programmes to get to the ads.
Each line perfect; she is her own best editor.
She sings lullabies and nations fall asleep,
the tanks on her lawn are all valet parked.
She wears adoring bees like a coat,
when she cuts herself she bleeds sequins.
She plans to rise and speak at her own funeral.
Each blind bend she meets is taken on two wheels,
she conceives destruction but will sue for peace.
Tired of being followed, she can detach her shadow,
she's fluent in profanity but doesn't read poetry.
Each kiss puts out a star or shifts its orbit,
she undresses; constellations vanish.
The fan vault of her laugh is heard by dogs alone.
I can't believe they haven't caught her yet.

Highland Recreation

In all these years, it's never been the silent burst of
daffodils
that crooks a finger to the spring
but the May Day firing-up of slot machines. Beneath the
hills

lithe coaches gather in dark pools, doors fluttering like
gills,
scales of sunlight glistening
on glass. Down among them are the darting shoals

of vans bringing boxes full of what this town has woken
for -
tablet, Talisker and Jimmy Shand -
their crabbit drivers smoking, a half-ear on the Celtic
score.

A stooping demi-monde in tartan peenie eyes us up and
wheezes
nae room left for us. Her cafe stands
mid-stream, between the banks of single malt and
macaroni cheese.

At six, high rollers dip for change and hit the penny
slots,
urge the swirling, winking coins
across the mirrored falls, or stake their shrapnel on
roulette.

We cross the dam which palms the loch away, while
supple salmon thrash
and swirl and form in urgent lines,
anticipate the opening of sluices, when stagnant grey
becomes a silver rush.

Grave Green

Damp in sleeping bags, in cooling light,
we opened up the tent to let it breathe,
welcoming the gathered noises in,
the demon hiss of distant traffic,
screeching beasts beyond the trees.
We caught the dark in musty traps,
stood well back and poked it with our sticks.

One boy, far from home at last,
snivelled as the darkness growled
through our soft mouths. It told us
of a place where once a kid
who swam too far into the lake
now lay, a crucifix of reeds above the spot
where he went under for the last time.
At dusk sometimes he rose, complete,
and swam again. By now the night
could tell how deeply we were lying.

Guy-ropes twanged like tendons,
the wind on the canvas like a roll of drums.
Once the fireglow forgot itself,
the night divided us into the boys
who scared themselves, and those
with stories we could never prove
were not just made from shadows.

Dawn unclothed itself, and smoke
was in each breakfast taste, the black-edged
bacon pan-fried over brimstone.

We climbed onto the bus, shoes thick
with heavy mud and cinders.
Alone up front, I heard him sniff,
saw fear and sleep in a crumbled glance,
cheeks dark with the ink from his tears.
Poor kid, he never stood a chance.

Dunbar Law

Today I coil a jute-rope round
the roosting hill above my rolling town,
tie it to my tail light, check
the tides and stretch my stiffened back.
I whiffle mud from off the frame,
nose my clanking pushbike south again,
across the contours. Love to say
how farms and hamlets wave me by,
but truth is, I could whistle through
at ninety and no-one would know.

Around the Neuk the folk are pale,
as landward gales numb up the face
of Fife, enamelled with a kingdom
crown right here. The wisdom
of the estuary calls in shrieks
of oystercatchers, pointed beaks
of pain which wheel and zoom.
It's here I set up my maroon
and hitch the rope around its trunk,
whisper solemn prayers for luck.

An unloved sign here illustrates
a line against the sky. I trace
the humps from Arthur's Seat, and mouth
their names. Bass Rock, and some way south
to fear and Lothians. Left a bit,
I'll send the fizzing rocket off to split
the difference between the hulks –

gaunt Cockenzie spires, the hunk
of lead-lined walls at stern Torness,
where Mausolus was laid to rest.

I light the fuse, and smell the sparks,
(instructions say to stand well back)
then boom! The shell divides the sky
from firth, and jerks the rope alive.
I watch the rocket racing, till it sputters,
dropping steeply over oil-flecked water,
see the rope go tight. I wind the slack
until it twangs, and then, not looking back
I set my face on bleak Dunbar
and tightrope-walk from Law to Law.

Air Band Radio

Each Friday, softened by wages,
he came home early
and lay dissolving his worker's grime,
the water rising and falling with his breath,
lapping in sympathy with the buzz
of his radio -
Not music but chatter
from the control tower,
the cocky few flying in for the weekend.
He knew their business -
diverted souls bound for Blackpool
or weathered out of Ringway,
in shells small enough to drop steeply
onto the green moss pasture
across the canal.

His sons passed out in rigid blue,
rank upon rank upon rank,
starting a life he might have wanted as his own.
He never saw himself in them
or them in him.

Crisply clothed in clean dusk air,
he watched alone from the turf below the tower,
stood at the wrong end of his binoculars,
his radio hissing gently on the car bonnet.
Noisy, tiny aircraft stooged above,
little wings, diamonds in the sky,
gleaming with every dip of their nose.
The mystery of their glass and silver skins

turned to china-cloth and plywood,
such a disappointment when you got close.

Surfacing

His rent is due. He works tonight.
The empty quarter calls. He leaps
from running boards, his eyes alight
and whistles while the city sleeps.
At bitter dawn he yawns and stands
reforming shapes from tarry breath,
heat meeting cold again. His hands
now gloved, his face is set like death,
thinking of her tightly cauled
in prickly sheets, her little head
as still as marble. Now she falls
in dreams of light, the lonely bed
as rough as gravel when she wakes.
She peels the sheets and lets the sun
warm through her bones. The moment breaks.
The night was cold, but now it's done.

His magic spell takes hold. A street
renewed, and he is leaving town.
They pass on stairs. He greets
her, going up, she coming down.

Wrong Time, Wrong Species

When I go out, I know
they are looking at me
as I trundle along
as I try to climb stairs
children point and
mummy stifles them
though they look away
I am still there

It started as a child
I knew I wasn't like the other boys
they played with sawn-off shotguns
and other warlike toys
while I wore full-length skirts
to glide across my bedroom floor
and coveted a plunger
from the corner hardware store

When, in my teens
my speech broke up
into syllables, clipped and steely
I knew that exams and a career
held nothing for me
but still I could not see clearly
what pattern was embroidered
in every cell and atom

I wanted to subjugate the free peoples
of the cosmos
and grind them into submission

encase my flesh in steel and plastic
exterminate the weak and the good
this was my evil vision
deep down, subconsciously
subcutaneously
I was born a Dalek

I would be eligible for mutation
on the National Health
but the waiting list was long
and I would have to live as a Dalek
for two years
to prove I was serious

we can mutate you said
a specialist disdainfully
but you must understand,
the process is irreversible

whatever the cost - do it I said
I will obey he replied

at the point where his prosthetics
fused with my genetics
I became

Wild West

He moves from spreadsheets to mean streets,
the rubble prairies of his town,
overflowing bins and tumbleweed.
The drinks in here are watered down
but cheap. He knocks one back and slackens
off his bootlace tie, draws smiley faces
in the sawdust with his foot. A blackened
scowl is thrown to thrill the ladies.

The cowgirls form in grids, the sway
of tasseled skirts and clod of boots
always a continent adrift. His joy
is in the dance, the squarest root,
each bar a perfect subroutine,
a formula, a certainty of codes
which repeat and then refine
themselves, smoothing out like tides.

Lit by phosphorescent smirr of night,
dad's old crombie glints with drizzle.
He is Alan Ladd in suit of lights,
his stetson and his smoking pistol
in a Tesco bag. A tombstone
in his guts, he rides the only stagecoach
in the west, afraid this town
ain't big enough for both of him.

Amateurs

Was it the heat? Today it got too much. They couldn't
bite
their tongues a moment more, and stood mid-aisle
squaring up like boxers under stuttering lights,
blunt curses forming in their minds. Perhaps she
recognised
his tight lips from the days when he would smile
with them, smile with all his face, and maybe realised
that even during sex he wouldn't look her in the eye,
that anger was the only thing that showed he was alive.

I shouldn't watch, although they don't seem skilled at
things,
she cuts him like a drunken surgeon, he so used to
crushing
her like biscuits in his hand. Neither one is crying
but I see an older woman dab a tear among the milling
shoppers. I push on through crowds, emerging
on the sunlit street, the smell of doughnuts cooking
signalling an end to famine, somewhere Stevie Wonder
playing,
proof that someone here knows what they're doing.

City Of The Dead

When my grave is broken up again
you will find the king of stone,
in favourite suit, and penny-eyed,
waxen skin and teeth of gold,
ring of bright hair round the bone,
his sense of humour for a shroud.

Surveying this necropolis
with scopes and lenses, double-blind,
you view the landfill site designs,
reserved for the unchecked remains
of you and yours, and now neck high
in bones, and what the worms reclaim.

You cannot cut new earth today,
though sextons dig and pile it high,
and stand around and lean on spades
as ranks of hearses wander by,
black tins of grief. The widow lays
a wreath of nettles on the grave.

At night the moon will move the tides,
and tides will boil to feed the sky.
There's always room up there for rain,
but down here we are full. We tried to save
a space for you, but could not find
a single plot to bear your Sunday name.

1969

I'm told they still hold séances
for celebrated spirits from those days,
the refugees from Woodstock, peering
into artificial darkness, listening for rasps
of breath or undiminished chords.
The fabled spirit bottled like youth dew,
the sweat from people we cannot be sure
will not re-form the band and tour again.

We watched the sky come down for good
and knew how this song ended. Altamont,
with hearts shot full of drink and anger,
headline act escaping in a hearse.
One watcher found the backpack she had carried
all these years was empty from the start,
and when the picture fizzled into herringbones
of static, turned to me and said through tears

I was there, and then, *We failed you. How we failed.*

Written Out

It isn't personal, it's ratings-led.
Dead storylines for you, and younger actors
on the scene, that's where it's at.
We cannot kill you off - the public
would not stand for that, and if
the ratings fall again, who knows,
We may decide to bring you back.
We cannot seem to make you speak in words
that dredge the soul, and so we fall back on
the lexicon of emptiness - you know the lines.

We're sending you to where the actors go
to wait for ravelled plots to bind again.
The call may come, a year, a decade,
who knows when? We'll fax the scripts.
Perhaps a funeral, you should be there.
Car draws up. It's you. In suit and shades
and studied grief, your shoulders fallen,
wife we've only heard about, a floral gift,
perhaps some kids. You're doing well.
It's good to have you back
just for a while. Maybe your brother
has a crash. His kidneys teeter, fail.
A donor sought. There's none about.
The monitor is bleeping out your name.

And while you're gone the cast will talk
of you sometimes with distant looks
in bar-room scenes or in the street.
How's your Andy? Phoned today,

he's doing fine. And me, spun off in Scotland
with a love that could restore your sight
or make the lame stand up,
content to think you're laughing still,
at crummy jokes I used to tell.

Salon Reg

They come to him from all across the town
to feel his hands, his casual suggestions
on their scalp, winkling out their secrets,
things they swore to take to distant graves.
He's combing through the dirty strands,
the scales of guilt and smoke of envy,
teasing them while squeezing out the mousse,
then setting them below a radiant heat.
Sometimes, as his scissors nimbly click,
he notes the way his own hair parts,
reversed in mirrors, unfamiliar.
The scandalous clippings at his feet
are taken home to stuff his pillows,
a comfort in his wild and frantic slumber.

Shower head in hand, he sprays fake pearls
across her head and neck, bends down, shares
another secret he has gleaned, and whispers
through the gloom *is that hot enough for you?*

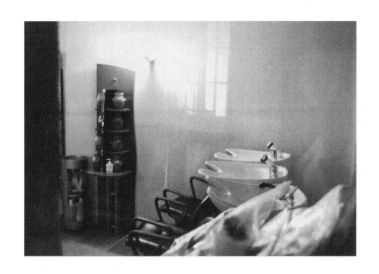

Let The Strobe Light Up Them All

Cold sore girl lights up a queue,
a glinting ironmonger's face,
talks of halter-necks and blowjobs,
laughs and rolls her eyes right back.
Friend is blank as a satellite dish,
flicking lighter flame, obsessed.
Smoke makes talons, claws the air
drenched with bootlegged scent, kebabs.
Clammy breezeblocks hold them firm,
air between them shimmying
to muffled beats, a languid thump,
sounds to charm their tattooed snakes
coiling up in secret places.
Wired-up bouncers, shirts too small,
cruise the line like guards in war films,
basilisks with shaded gaze,
thrilled by screams or whine of tyres,
tinted headlights, scorching rubber,
low-gear gunning past the column
four or five times every hour.
Boy with sovereign ring is claiming
territory with his voice,
random noise, his declarations,
love and hate, to see and have,
to live and die and know the difference.
I'm as old as lunar landings.

Awfie Stourie

An artisan arrived to smash the wall
between two peaceful rooms.

His coldest chisel broke rough rusks
of brick, sent each one zooming.

I winced through every hammer-smack,
the marrow leaking from my bones.

After his infernal symphony,
he deemed the carnage was complete.

We spoke across each other for a while,
neither of us looking at the mess.

"It's awfie stourie...". Yes, it was.
"Eh'm a wee bit clarty...". Right again.

I noted how his cheery diminutions
sped the strokes of brush on dustpan,

had me whistling through the Bluebell Polka,
clearing up the aftermath of what could be

a wee axe-murderie,
a wee bloodbathie,
a wee holocaustie.

Marmite

A food for kids? This myth persists.
I was weaned for years on it.
Now I see the shape of the jar,
and ache to stroke its fertile curves,
child-bearing hips, a trove
of bitter treacle, black as a vat
of roadside tar.

I know some fearless types
drink metal polish straight
and chain-smoke crack from dirty pipes.
When offered Marmite, hear their palates fizz
and watch their grey lips pucker.
See them spit out ragged balls
of half-chewed bread, amazed some nutter
could eat that stuff and live.

Now, my palate's tempered
in the furnaces of a thousand
curry houses, every one a challenge,
but when I dip into this
bottomless pot and slide
the laden knife across my teeth,
there's still that jolt, that flash of
electricity, down to the hungry roots beneath.

Expiry

She must have been reaching inside
the frozen display, like hunching over
a communion rail, awaiting the elements.

Ten items or less wrote their own list;
Dog food, liver salts, one pork chop,
bruised apples, beyond the power
of dentures, frost on frozen peas
leeching into blue skin.

Supervisor, conjured by tannoy,
tabard rustling, squeezed for a pulse
like a housewife palpating fruit,
unripe wrist in her grip ribbed
with tendons, like a celery stick.

Final breath cast over markdowns
in an aisle that no-one visited,
loyalty points irredeemable now.

Dan Dare Is Dead

I blasted off from my only world,
its craters deep as pockmarks,
a dim crust sprinkled with unfurled
star patterns plucked from dark
and strewn across the counterpane.
I lay itching, safe in candlewick
and dreaming of my footprints on the plains
of Venus, space lanes thick
with rickety rocket ships all manned
by fearless pilots from the war,
dapper in their silken monogrammed
pyjamas, square of purpose and of jaw.

All grammar-schooled young chaps
knew Englishmen would have their say
at last, but modern pens drew newer maps
which hinted that we might have lost our way
in traffic. The dead weight of an empire gone,
we saw our decent selves in stranger skies
beyond the spinning of a British sun.
For every fall there ought to be a rise,
opposite and equal, a better sort
of empire, an English-speaking universe.
Despite the yanks and reds, we rather thought
a Cambridge man would get there first.

Straight Man

She always bought the presents
from a catalogue, sweetly meant
but more off-target every year.
She never let you sign the cards,
afraid that you'd forget yourself
and swear, and leave them spoiled.
In winter, when she faltered
you would wander in for tea.
We'd never seen the two of you
apart, the double act about to end,
the straight man and the droll,
one working up a solo act.

The meal had lost its taste. The gingham
crinkled, damp. You pushed the plate away
and rose as small as you had ever stood,
embarrassed finally by tears.
We cried as well, confused. You went
off-script to make one mis-timed joke,
used lines we thought you hadn't learned,
and stumbled through it till the end.
The act cut short, we learned too late
the thing that all the comics know -
In this business, when you go,
always leave them wanting more.

Wife tells pop star: 'It's the monkey or me'

*A German pop star is trying to salvage his marriage after his wife
left him when he moved a monkey into their marital home. Werner
Boehm was introduced to the 10-year-old female baboon while
filming a music video. He said: "It was love at first sight. The
monkey is extremely musical and can even play the piano. We're on
the same wavelength."*

He brought a monkey home,
a beast, one aeon short of humanity.
He swore to civilise it,
still it ate flowers, pissed in corners,
reached greedily for my breasts.
The small bed sheltered me,
until I found them lying together,
our kingdom of tenderness
now a mess of writhing limbs.

He asked me to lie with them,
gave their fun a harmless name.
I could not tell one from the other.
We wrestled, for his pleasure -
I felt hairy hands upon me, but whose?
A cultured touch now clumsy,
artless groping, no use at all.
His was a jealous animal now,
beating his chest for primacy.

I had been loved so lavishly before,
dignity in every union,
but this was beyond duty.
His tongue, prehensile as his tail,

clutched me, saying
You are still welcome, lover
but if you want the man
you must accept the monkey.

New World Order

Some claim to see the micro-pulse
of blood, or bird migration paths
like watermarks in star-filled skies,
or make out chains of cancer cells
from airborne views of stubbled fields.
I imagine there are rules about these things
derived from chilly mathematics.
In theory we can peel away the mundane
layers, take the look in someone's eye
and boil it down to quark and meson.

I thought I saw these rhythms in you,
humdrum cycles of unbending time,
grow up, give birth, get old, die.
You couldn't know how you were made
from flakes of stardust, accidentally,
no room for the unquantifiable
emotions that defy investigation.

Those of us who have a way with words
can sometimes look so hard we miss it -
someone running just to feel the wind,
or shouting just to hear their voice,
jumping up to feel the pull back down,
leaving us, who want each life to be a poem,
wordless when it matters most.

Saturday

Each day we punch the ticking clocks
and send our wives again to sieve the Clyde
for little flakes of gold to turn to coins,
the currency accepted at the turnstile rack.
The north stand is a mountainside,
an iron mound of twisted anchor chains

lit up by candle-power and cigarettes.
The grinding roars and flint-faced jeers
are swelling into chants and calls for blood,
their blood, our blood. Not hollow threats,
but promises distilled from night-black beer,
of how they'd kill us if they could.

In the lull between attacks, the elders draw
the young ones in with stories slick with brilliantine,
their fat fists clenched in victory. They talk about
the frostbit night they saw McGrory score,
and the plague of bottles visited upon the other team
the night they put the lights of Glasgow out.

Then all at once, black wings above a lake of noise
throw doomy shadows on the floodlit waves.
The whistle blows. An old man goes in hard,
dark passions in his scything, slicing voice,
bares his gravestone teeth and utters *Jesus saves...*
but Lennox taps the rebound in from seven yards.

The game goes on forever. We raise up our bitter songs
and walk together, strong in columns, arm in arm,

dispersing into tenements and sandstone lives.
Tomorrow we will feel the wafer on our tongues,
say our prayers and meekly cast our holy charms.
By Monday, we will just be husbands to our wives.

Cheeky Devil

I am public enemy number one.
I shout, dance on benches
scuffle on civic furniture
push sticks into pram wheels at rest
leave stones in exhaust pipes
imagining expanding, exploding cars
kick at holes in fences
throw a new ball into roses
to hear the hiss as thorns pierce its heart.
I keep trophies – a shedful
of burst footballs
stringless rackets
chainless bikes.

Jennie Lee by Robert Capa

Daughters, hear the truth. Back then,
no pit was deep enough for diamonds,
none would strike a match
for fear of fire-damp.
The roar of the conveyor belt
drove girls from blackened homes
in Fife, their coughing fathers
burning out like cinders.

She was caught by gales that swept
across the steppes, to rattle windows
on collective farms, yearning for
the gusts of revolution.
She broke the ceilings in a ruin,
breathed on plaster till it cracked,
then helped to mix the sand
with the cement to build us up again.

The artist, bleak in his fatigues
and listening out for shells,
is sizing up the shot. His art
is in the truth, his propaganda
is the likeness of a better world
already here, if we could only see
its levelling of light and dark,
its socialism of the eye.

Keep-Net

Perhaps we are too stupid to know,
but when that flashing feather
dips down beyond the mirror,
it's a wise one that can tell it
from a struggling fly at its end.
Dim shadows on the bank, not trees,
but just as still except for serpent arms
waving like a slow dance, back and to,
beyond hammered glass.
In the faint wake of the fly
there are tiny ripples,
incantations, ritual words,
little murmurs splashing like gravel,
sinking to the bed of the stream.
We cannot lie in our hollows forever.

From where we swim now
the water flows across us just the same,
but where once there was a world
now we bump against fins.
At every skipping turn, we find friction,
nylon snags, scraped scales.
When the shade deepens
he starts to pack away his day,
and the water is chilled beyond cold.
The catches on the tackle box click.
I have to believe that I will be thrown back.

Hypermetropia

Sit down you say, not facing me,
but nodding at the hump of leatherette
crouching down against the mustard wall.
It buzzes like a mercy seat,
and tingles with the borrowed spoor
of someone else's thighs.

Your tests should all be simple -
should I make my eyes perform
or make the blindness bigger?
I cannot blink the blur away.
Your tears are thick you say.
I wonder how you know.

I hear you rustle as you bend
to me. I fix my eyes like glass.
Your breath is hot against my cheek,
and leaves a brutal scorchmark
with each hiss, close enough
to be a lover. Is this where we kiss?

Your instrument clicks thinly
as you peer into each corner,
but your scope can't see the image
on my retina, above me, lost in passion.
Beyond the smoothness of your shoulder
I can read the letters on your chart

W

    H   A

  T   H   A

 P   P   E   N

S   N   O   W   ?

Interloper

A slideshow is hosted for a yellowing
clan in a Californian suburb.
I am there, over-exposed beneath
the bougainvillea, squinting
out-of-focus by the winter palace.

In a Tokyo room I wander into shot,
head in a guide book, laughing.
Video cuts to a shot of a man
pointing a video at a man pointing
a video back at him and I am caught
in their merciless crossfire.
Look! A third camera on the grassy knoll
but I will not be edited out.

Herr X opens a glossy pack of snaps.
Over the shoulder of his roll-necked wife
I grin as alabaster and bronze fuse, tumbling
opal drops over our heads, thinking
Jesus, look at his Jesus boots.
I did not ask to come into your home,
you brought me here.

The Gymnast

I cut her picture from the paper -
that grubby smile transferred to fingers -
spoke to her while making beds.
She spoke back in my breaking voice,
disfigured by her leotard,
smeared with smiles and studied joy,
hormones held in trust for her
until the medals came back home.
A swaying reed, not buffeted
by awkward, tumbling years,
now insolently bending back
to meet new pain with dogged force.
A perfect sister, slight but sturdy,
hands aching now with bravery
and leathery with friction.
She strikes a deal with gravity
then pushes at its margins.
Not looking down, she walks on glass,
is caught again, mid-leap.

La Nozze di Miss Italia

While swooping stage lights
play across the meatless ribs
of hollow catwalk beauties,
lurex-skinned and bottle-brown,
I watch a simple pageant
out beyond the main event -
children learning from their peers,
mastering their sultry arts,
swinging hips and tossing hair.

Beside the plastic pot-plants
they are parodies of flowers.
An old man with a clipboard
sees the snowdrops in their hair
and says, without a thought,
how spring keeps coming
earlier each year.

Dysfunctional

He never saw himself in need of therapy
It's only natural for your urges to diminish,
the woman said, *but sex should be a joyful symphony.*
Too right, he thought. *Pathetique. Unfinished.*

Careers Advice

To show respect I flew my trousers
at half-mast, tightened up my tie.
Her eyes were dimmed by sherry
saying *I am here to help you*
but you have to help yourself.
A cloud came past the window and
the sudden dusk distorted her,
and she was young again, her life
a jamboree of learning. I was urged
to yield to industry. A leaflet drew
my picture and described my future years
in overalls, content but slightly puzzled.

Darkness came. I watched her drive away,
her headlights knifing through the drizzle,
shale leaping crisply from her thrumming tyres.
I saw myself through her eyes, wondered
if she was more worried about me
than I was about her. Ducking back
into the shadows, merging with graffiti,
I felt her leaflet crumpling already
in my blazer pocket.

Inch'allah

Come cluster bombs and fall on sand
where stone age people dwell.
If friendly fire gets out of hand,
God willing, you will understand
the Testament we tell.

The *chop* of rotors choked your calls
to build and clothe and feed,
but speeches spun in gilded halls
or shaking cans in shopping malls
are hardly what you need.

By cloak of dust and winter's chill
the target is selected.
We watch them moving to the kill,
the truth is laser-guided, still
some signals are rejected.

Avoid all clichés once again,
(for clichés are complacent).
Can we get God on News At Ten,
or interviewed on CNN?
You'll have to ask his agent.

The trails reflected in these skies
are etched by truths colliding.
Can viewers tell the truth from lies,
when set before their hawkish eyes?
Our phone poll is deciding...

Were pestilence and power cuts
predicted in your Scriptures?
If bones are crunching underfoot
we may not run the story, but
for Christ's sake get some pictures.

The cameras looked deep inside
each firefight we saw
We let the ratings be our guide,
we chose a side and *Havoc*! cried,
let slip the fog of war.

Corryvreckan

An oilskinned roughneck eyed us up
and promised us the sober thrills
of speed and boiling tides and swells.
His jet-boat whipped like light across
the waveless sound. Aboard, we gripped
each other, scared the stiffish breeze
might prise us from our open seats
and push us down to drown us in the deep.
A spew of fulmars streaked across our wake,
familiars of the promised demon of the straits.

The engines cut, we drifted out
between the tense black knuckles
of the islands, both expecting to be wowed
by swirling eddies, whitened lips of water
round a whirlpool, bottomless,
the gulping of a monster's throat,
draining down then fiercely bubbling up.
Instead, a sheet of troubled glass,
the serpent-hissing of the ebbing tide
and other inconclusive signs of Hell.

The ocean chose today to hide its malice,
not perform its canny tricks to order,
staying calm when every instinct was to rage.
Then, later on, your lapping sighs, your
sea-grey eyes half closed against
the coming storm, the spinning sky,
the water filling up the space between us,
then, the swirling gurgle of the plug,

the water draining from the bath.
We shiver, like this warmth is all we have.

She Just Came Out Of Nowhere

We were almost sweethearts
for a week or two one summer,
but when the school was finished
I joined the queue to sign her blouse,
biro scrawl embroidery from boys
who said that she was easy.
We stood in line, all threatening
to be the one to sign the patch of cloth
that rose and fell with every breath.

Years before, her silly sister died
beneath a car on a loveless road
that ran too close to auntie's house.
Mothers tutted in the butchers,
muttered that it had to happen
sometime to some mother's child.
I saw her once beside the sign
the cops put by the spot, counting cars
and writing down their numbers.
Accident here. Can you help?

I Am An Exile Now

I am an exile now, making a brief
return to share the latest clannish rites,
form human chains and share in grief,
or wave a happy couple off into their night
of nights, her dress too tight across the front,
the boozy groom forever loosening his tie.
The cava flows, and mushroom vol-au-vents
are all it takes to draw exotic sighs
from granny. Staring at a photo on the wall
she says *I'm happy with my lot*,
and then, without a pause, *they call*
them good old days, but they were not.

S-Bahn

You have to remember,
as a junior soldier
I had obligations
to go where they sent me-
to a city of vetoes,
cold and blockaded,
lit up by slogans
and dubbed into English.

We couldn't get near you
without valid papers.
Partitioned and quartered
by reinforced concrete,
Your cauterized roadways
were pockmarked and cratered`,
while up in the towers,
the laughter of snipers.

You told me *remember*
There's U-bahn and S-bahn.
The 'U' is for using,
The 'S' is verboten.
Who were the drivers?
Who punched the tickets?
I thought you were joking,
but no-one was laughing.

Your underground network
was annexed and severed,
straddling sectors,

cutting through freedom,
No warnings of crossings.
no passwords, no checkpoints,
no hiss of pneumatics,
no station announcements,

But that was the eighties,
when nothing was settled,
the soldiers got weary,
of watching each other.
You patched up your squabbles,
went back to your partner,
I danced at your wedding,
but you are still dancing.

The Testament of St John Vianney

This is the new orthodoxy; anyone will tell.
The plasma screen runs hot, and I lie still
below the peaks of popcorn, dull as ash,
stalked by hulking lava flows of Häagen Dazs.

Likewise, after supper I take the rinsed-out cup,
flecked with Special Brew, let the sticky sofa wrap
me in a shroud of wine-stained leatherette,
and lie in state with my Sex And The City box set.

There are no fixed devotions to perform,
no litany or lectionary. But see the signs around my
home,
the face of Jesus formed from patterns on the wall,
the pinging of the microwave an altar bell.

This at last is purity: an indolence of thought
as well as deed, empty of lust or hate or doubt.
I am eternally unworried, unfocused, unresolved.
I was not listening when you called.

And when at last the cushion sores merge into one,
the listless child emerges from the man.

Beating the Retreat

It's on again - that trailer for the winter
where sneaky outdoor spiders, fat on summer flies,
relocate their business of entrapment and embalming.
Crows are nutmeg on the custard of the sky
while geese are magnetised in martial V's,
striking out for lake beds and savannahs.

I grease the bikes and chain them both together
in the dark. The outdoor chairs go in the loft,
to curl in foetal poses for nine months.
The garden splutters, acts as if it's still July,
with stunted little plants I cannot name.
Disturbed, I watch my wife with secateurs,
and note the zeal of her castrating snips.
The vapour trails thin out above us, turbojets
are throttled back, as stewardesses stash
their kevlar tabards for another year.

An autumn's coming. Maybe it's our last. I heard
some Colonel on the telly say retreat is just advancing
in a different direction. The sun is gone for good,
come inside now, come inside.

The Cyclist

In the dark
the gear-clank and click of rusting chain
will prick his sleep.

He thinks of all the times when, tired,
he slipstreamed her,
sheltered in the pliant, fragile lee of

her pipe-cleaner body.
He would always be the one to fall behind,
gamely hauling up

the deadweight of himself, while she,
a streak of energy,
burned grooves along the road beyond.

He knows the layers
of her world, the soft-edged rainbow stripes
of sky, then cloud,

her downward smile, the grass, the certain
tarmac strip, the blurred
black sunglass frame, the pinhead glow of sweat

on puffed-out cheeks.
Across the saddle of the rise he hears a car,
sees its outward swerve,

too close around the space that he defends.
His muscles pump.
then silence, nearly, just the *tick tick tick*

of lazy pedals,
whip of wind, precursor of a siren that will not,
in this world, ever stop.

~

He stows her broken bike upon the rack.
It will do for spares,
when tyres lose their air and spokes deform.

A year from now
it hangs there in the garage, half digested.
His bike like a mantis

swallowing its mate, a necessary meal if one
is to survive
the empty road, the pointless journey on.

Via Dolorosa

In a lull between the bombers
someone passed a bag of ham
to him. He knew the risks, the fines,
the faces of black marketeers,
but still he took the midnight tram,

his duffle coat a crushing weight.
And, sure his little contraband
was bulging, forming guilty lines,
he scurried through delinquent streets,
the bag stigmata on his hands.

Spectral footsteps chased him down
as streets conspired with darker lanes
to take his soul and turn him round.
Across the bridge: the black canal
below called out his filthy name.

He felt the footsteps in his head,
his hands curled tighter round the sack.
One heave and then a hollow splash,
the moon on ripples, then, no trace.
He turned. No-one was at his back.

Sometimes he will repeat those steps.
He even stops to see that place
and wonders if a hand will rise,
and thrust his crime into the world.
The water's still. He walks away.

Ne Me Quitte Pas

I met a man who said that he had written
down a playlist for divorce, each dirge engaged
to bind her heart with wire. The pain of splitting
up the vinyl, the tearing of their single page
in two was hard. She'd marvelled at his calm
the time that she got drunk and smashed
a seventy-eight, how he pressed his palms
together, held her gaze, refilled her glass.
Secretly he drew a goatee and moustache
on Joni Mitchell's 'Ladies Of The Canyon' cover.
She bought it on his say-so, hated it. The Clash
were more her thing, serve her right, nothing clever.

The playlist rolled. She went upstairs to pack
as Waits and Cohen mumbled in support.
His selfish angel cautioned *Change the stupid locks,
make her leave her key*, but then his thoughts
returned to Brel, whose salt and honey tongue
was tracing shapes on her, whose conjured lover's
tears were spoiling it for all of us, whose grating song
was making promises she knew he never could deliver.

Painful Life

"New figures show that the misery memoir market doubled from £12m in 2005 to £24m last year, with up to 10 new titles vying to be top of the glums each month. The top-selling misery memoir in the UK - Behind Closed Doors by Jenny Tomlin - shifted 278,000 copies in 2006, more than six times the number sold by last year's Booker Prize winner, The Inheritance of Loss by Kiran Desai". (Anthony Barnes, Independent Newspaper, Sunday, 4 March 2007)

I was not drugged to sleep each night. The gravel
in my knee is a reminder of the time I came
off Robert Fowler's bike. The doctor marvelled
that a break could be so clean, but knew the games
that children play could snap an arm like that.
I did not fear the landing light or footsteps at the door.
The egg-shaped purpling lump was from a cricket bat
swung round too hard. I wasn't made to live with whores
or give my body nightly to old men with tattooed hands.
I ran away from home for half an hour. I cried a bit.
There's nothing I'm not telling you, dear friend.
I grew up having fun. I am still loved. That's it.

Eternity Ring

In a secret ceremony, I presented her
with a circle wound from wires of brass,
inset with cubic zircons, chips of stone,
a twisted girdle, universal and complete.
Of course, she left it lying on a lonely strand,
while paddling. A guilty breaker covered it,
slunk back, ashamed, then carried it far out,
beyond the shore, into the gullet of a cold Atlantic fish.

We returned each night to comb for missing gold,
and other jewels of the lost, knowing these
were not the treasures that the sea gives up.
Perhaps one day we'll settle to our supper,
a careless bite will knock my crown right off.
Here is the ring, eternal and untarnished, rolled along
by shiftless currents, safe and shiny in the belly
of a silver darling, now miraculously washed up here
among the lukewarm chips. We never understood
the indecisive ebb and flow of things, but believed
in a love like Bogart and Bacall's, the sweet and bitter
both the same. If you find this poem, or the ring,
please keep it; it's too late for us.